FALLS LAKE:
Swimming in History

poems by

Faith S. Holsaert

Finishing Line Press
Georgetown, Kentucky

FALLS LAKE:
Swimming in History

Copyright © 2020 by Faith S. Holsaert
ISBN 978-1-64662-199-6   First Edition
All rights reserved under International and Pan-American Copyright Conventions. No part of this book may be reproduced in any manner whatsoever without written permission from the publisher, except in the case of brief quotations embodied in critical articles and reviews.

ACKNOWLEDGMENTS

Landscape, erasure, Imam Jamil Al Amin at Butner, Walking with Ancestors, appeared at *Barzakh Magazine*, June 2019, https://www.barzakh.net/spring-2019-poetry/2019/6/3/three-poems-1

Cover Art: Jim Lee, Bamboo Turtle Studio, Durham, NC

Jim Lee is a Durham, NC photographer/artist who draws much of his inspiration from nature and his love of science. His work ranges from still life photographs of found objects to small 3D sculptural pieces, some of which are incorporated into his photos.

New Gourd Wars 007 shows the areas of conflict among different species of mold as they compete for nutrients on the surface of a gourd. It can be seen to illustrate themes of settlement and appropriation which are at the heart of this collection of poems.

Publisher: Leah Maines
Editor: Christen Kincaid
Author Photo: Vicki L. Smith
Cover Design: Elizabeth Maines McCleavy

Printed in the USA on acid-free paper.
Order online: www.finishinglinepress.com
            also available on amazon.com

Author inquiries and mail orders:
Finishing Line Press
P. O. Box 1626
Georgetown, Kentucky 40324
U. S. A.

Table of Contents

Osprey 1

Out Cheek Road 2

Surface 4

Danette at Falls Lake 5

Adviso 6

Wild 7

Back and Forth 8

Open Water 9

Landscape, an erasure 10

Imam Jamil Abdullah Al-Amin at Butner 13

Walking with Ancestors 16

Plantain 21

Body of Knowledge 22

Dam the Rivers 24

Found Poem 27

Snake Like a Wreath 28

Hurricane Season, 2017 29

Schooled 33

Winter 34

Osprey

from the boundary pole
the osprey launches

she drifts in blue and white
displaying her house cat belly

a plane rumbles from
left to right   and is gone

the hawk hangs above
speculative

she sees the road
she sees the snake
she sees the unhatched turtles
who slumber in the earth

Out Cheek Road

forty-five miles per hour
industrial chain link
brick church in a curve
15 miles per hour for tracks
BBQ place on right
a man walks to his car
and he is Black

snaky curve left
small houses with
short straight drives
one flamboyant patch of orange lilies
gas station sells propane
and deer corn
once I saw a Black man there
and same for the crossroads
with the four-way stop
the crossroads with BP gas
shiny roofs above the pumps

slow at Clayton to let
drivers turn toward Southern High

where is last summer's giant confederate flag?
when it says Heritage Restaurant is "heritage" code for white?

the cinderblock houses larger
white woman manning a riding mower
road to left blocked
where would I be if I took that detour?
needn't concern me

the two-story farmhouse
windows busted out, siding falling off
porch gone
in the sideyard a tribe of
grazing goats dappled in the sun

is the farmhouse being restored or torn down?
what is to become of the goats?

Surface

dimpled brown water
rocked and wind blown
bowls of waves hold
enormity of blue and white sky

Dannette at Falls Lake

above the lake
Dannette with two enns and two tees
lies back in her bright blue hammock
her children recline against her
all three float
her body the bosom of the lake

Adviso

Katina and I will take her dog Shamrock to swim.
This is not quite legal but possible if we arrive early.

I say on the phone, *There is a health advisory—unsavory matter.*
I don't say, *Actually, fecal matter.*

She texts, *I'm concerned about the health adviso.*
I text, *I swim regardless. It is after all a kind of funky lake.*

I don't say, *I am never happier than when I step
into the water and free of the earth's pull.*

Katina says, *Please don't. Your skin is your largest organ.
All that you touch your liver must filter. Please don't.
You are precious,* she says so.

Maybe I'll skip today, because I love Katina
and because she said *precious*,
but tomorrow, tomorrow
I will go without her even though.
Even though she also actually said,
We need you.

Wild

I lay down phone and towel,
tear open velcro'd sandals. Nearby,
a mother's encampment—
floaties and towels and cooler.

Her baby calls
not-words to the lake.
A boy up to his chest in water
laughs at the middle girl.
Hurry, he calls
and she calls, *I'm waiting for Mami.*

Without my glasses the trees soften
and inhabit the sky more entirely.
Air warm on my shoulders
and bare back.
Soon: into the lake.

The mother looks up.
Soon: deeper and
deeper into the lake.
My feet will lift off.
She waves toward the boy, the girl,
the baby who has plopped onto her bottom.
We're kind of wild, she says.

Half naked I step into not particularly
clean water and let it uplift me.
I say, *Aren't we all?*
looking back over my warm shoulder.

Back and Forth

In the lake, I walk and run
back and forth,
left step, right step, left step
minute upon minute upon minute

A boy, maybe four years old—quick and self assured
and stumbling, all at once—
wades toward me. "Hello," he calls
across the space that separates us,
he in the shallow—he can touch bottom—
and I chest deep further out.
His eyes yearn to reach me with such force—
across my mother gone decades before
my brown haired fearless sister when she was four.
I think this one with the ambitious eyes
and precarious hold, this baby is not stopping.
He will trip and go under before I can reach him.
A look from him, deep and longing
before he turns back.
I walk and run on, a quarter hour to go.

Open Water

they say
in *man-made* lakes
do not swim
in open water
trees still standing from *before*—
underwater hazard

Landscape, an erasure

> *an erasure of EB White's "Once More to the Lake"*
> *with apologies to students I made read this*
> *when I didn't hear what my students were saying.*
> *because I insisted it was beautiful writing*
>
> *in my 70s, paring reveals landscape as race and class*

I.
1904 … father rented … and took … and … rolled … in success
that lake … one month … placidity … the woods … old haunts

sweet outdoors … long shadows … cathedral
remote … primeval

I …
the boy … was I … was my father …
silently … the dragonflies … came …
dislodging … years

exactly enchanted … lake
constant and trustworthy body
minnow with its … individual shadow

There had been no years

II.
two-track road
… lay … in the sun
loosened … plantains … weeds

dry noon … steamed
heat and hunger and emptiness

pie ...
waitresses ... country girls been to the movies
seen ... pretty girls with clean hair

III.
indelible ... fade proof ... unshatterable
sweet ... juniper ... without end
the design ... innocent and tranquil
flagpole and the American flag
floating ... escaping

newcomers ... *common*

IV.
to me ... remembering ... jollity and peace and goodness
farm ... smell of pine
smiling farmer
father's ... authority

V.
wrong ... the sound ... years moving
nervous ... outboard ... jarred

inboard ... an ingredient of summer sleep
fluttered ... purred

outboards ... petulant ... whined
my boy ... single-handed mastery

the ... old ... heavy flywheel
you could have it eating out of your hand...
... cool nerve

VI.
endlessly ... accumulated heat ... swamp drift ... rusty screens
steamboat that had a rounded stern like the lip of a Ubangi [said casual and not self conscious]
moonlight ... mandolin
doughnuts ... fig newtons ... Beeman's gum ... I ...

VII.
thunderstorm ... climax
darkening ... premonitory
gods licking their chops
my groin felt the chill of death

Imam Jamil Abdullah Al-Amin at Butner

At exit 186 on I-85, you may exit south
and drive through farmland
u-pick strawberries
tree stump removal
Cedar Creek Pottery
and wind up at Sandling Beach on Falls Lake,

or you can turn north toward Butner, NC,
small town home to institutions:
central regional hospital, a psychiatric *facility*
butner federal correctional *center*
butner federal medical *center*.

"The voice of Black Power," H. Rap Brown
or Jamil Abdullah Al-Amin,
might have been whisked
in an armored vehicle
up the exit I take to swim,
but he would have been turned left.

I would have turned right
at the gas station with a sign for seed corn
and left at the next junction,
past the field with three gleaming horses
right at the barn and down 50
past the chickens for sale—
pet or meat—
and the unfriendly convenience store
which sells propane.

Transferred from ADX Florence
supermax in Colorado,
where the Imam had been incarcerated
seven storeys below ground—
so close to the heart of the earth
so alone.

Seven years of sensory deprivation,
enough time for an infant
to be born, learn to walk,
and enter elementary school,
and more years than that.

I park where the shadows extend
to cover my car.
The water is brown
and cool on my feet.

He languished on the far side
of the continent.
When he fell ill, our letters:
Stop execution by medical neglect.

Two brown-skinned teenagers
stand to their shoulders
in water, arms around one another,
unaware of the pair of white
egrets gliding in tandem above.

At Butner, bone marrow revealed
smoldering myeloma
for this Imam whose words
were once fire—
Violence is American as Cherry Pie.

I put in my three back and forths,
an hour of walking and swimming
breathing in someone's
pork smoldering on a grill,
passing the embracing teens
six times in all.

Sjogren's syndrome:
severe pain
swelling of jaw and ankles
skin discoloration
broken teeth,
nearly evicting him from
his incarcerated body.

The three thwarted rivers
that are Falls Lake
permeate the soil of Butner
and finger its culpability.

He is the turn left and north to Butner
and I the turn right to the lake.
He will stay behind those walls
that foundation touched by the lake
until the authorities say otherwise.
I will go home and shower and make dinner

I go to the lake and swim unfettered.
He has been incarcerated at *the law's* say so.

He will outlast them.

Walking with Ancestors
> *Julia Sangodare Roxanne Wallace films the story of formerly enslaved*
> *people as they prepare for their first camp meeting as free people*

we enter the plantation
and park before a backdrop of trees
Julia Sangodare has summoned us

she can see each of us
      can see us in the film which has not yet been shot

solitary white woman, I walk across the grass.
I wear gray thrift store skirt to my ankles
we will not talk about how hot it is, in this polyester skirt
summer   Eno River Basin   2015

sitting in the unglazed window
15 year old Ida has emerged whole from bondage
and smiles down upon us

community making a way out of no way
an act of imagining then
as Sangodare dreams now

what traditions to carry into freedom
what traditions to leave behind

the people sing
    take me to the water
    take me to the water

Sangodare has named the girl in the window Ida,
for Ida B. Wells anti-lynching voice of fire
    in this life—high school, PSAT's—
    the super heroes she draws day and night
    at birth her mother gave her a revolutionary's name
        Assata daughter and sister
        of women who dream and who smile in flames

people   *dance*

the plantation—trees and hiding spots
and blackberry brambles
and weathered outbuildings—
once occupied
—that last word—
thirty thousand acres of river basin
trees shorn to afford an unobstructed
view of *the quarters*

now crept over by trees and brush

Julia Roxanne Sangodare Wallace.
past, present and future in a name
      green gold blue gossamer   dragonfly
        spirit spirit   black lake at night

the land acquired in 1776
—birth of a stolen nation
where once people and confederations and languages thrived—
plowed to receive tobacco and *cereal grains*,
worked to feed stock

nine hundred enslaved African people
nine hundred
lived here

after emancipation family members
post letters and handbills, searching for missing
husbands, wives mothers and fathers their children
like now

on topo map lacework of elevated crowns
and low points necklaced   dense weave of brown
      today Ida who is Assata
        Kynita who loves Afiya who is Assata's mother

       Mayto who is Sangodare's father Waylon in Sunday shirt
       and the person who is Sangodare's mother Anne
       in full white skirt and hand sewn white blouse
       her head wrapped in white
the lake fingers into the lacework
who knows the original configuration
on paper the lake water is unblemished pale green
lying in beds created by engineers
covering ancient trails
—shelving knowledge still there—
       a drone captures a waterfall's cascade
       deep inside the weave
       Alexis Pauline Gumbs firebrand who loves
       Sangodare leaps into the clearing
       body arched, feet high above the ground
       exclamation points
       Alexis Pauline Gumbs lands precisely as a damsel fly
just so

i am a walk-on under a voice-over
a white woman in Quaker drab who stands
on the porch of the general store
she reads aloud to those seeking stolen family
my seconds below another' voice pass quickly
the middle of a story which will continue
past Assata's sixteenth birthday,
past her graduation from high school,
beyond her journey west to college

2018 courtroom it is that story again
the great seal of the State of North Carolina.
1775 draped female figures of Liberty and Plenty (white)
       In the film: Harriett: Anne (Anthonette) Elix Wallace
       mother of Sangodare

Courtroom B has its choreography
of white judge and mostly white lawyers,
mumbling as we watch
    Mayto (the preacher): Rev. Waylon R. Wallace
    the father of Sangodare
to set the court's calendar, we listen to the judge's vacation schedule
    Hyacinth: Dannette Sharpley
    mother of Baez and Mimi
the bailiff brings in Black defendants
cuffed, shackled, jump-suited
    voice of grown Ida: Iya Osunfunke Omisade Burney-Scott
    practitioner of contemporary Ifa
    mother of Che and Taj
with its white liberty and white plenty
slavery occupied land to bring white plenty
slavery thought to steal liberty of
    Ida of
    Harriett of
    Mayto of
    Hyacinth
courtrooms steal lives
    Pauline: Dr. Alexis Pauline Gumbs
    love evangelist and poet
    loves and is loved by Sangodare

It is windy at Falls Lake
water in dark troughs
white capped crests

a heron works the sky
searching the depths
for life

people invent themselves
from day to day
and all the days going back to Africa
and all the days forward into a time
I can only ever imagine

Plantain
    (mostly found poem)

Settlers brought the seeds
impacted into the bottom
of their horses' hooves.

The common plantain known as
the white man's footprint
grows everywhere in the
continental united states,
in lawns and roadsides,
in grasses as I enter
Falls Lake State Park,
at the edge of woods
crowding the beach.

Also known as mother of herbs
her crushed leaves
can stem the flow of blood
or soothe the itch of poison ivy.

She has been known to
break through gravel
and crack street pavement
elbowing out from the rich soil beneath.

Body of Knowledge

I.
I walk my Jewish woman's white body into the lake
water gloves my body
water absorbs my wake

I know not much more than
what I find on google—
that peoples lived here.
Conventional wisdom says,
they disappeared without a trace.
I hear the name Okeneeche
I hear the name Tewa
I hear the name Saponi.
When I try to find which people
lived where the entries are
contradictory and confounding
> perhaps about the early people
> perhaps about the people today
> perhaps the names of languages
> and not the names of a people at all.

And on the way-cool tiny maps—
each people its own body of
green, red, purple, or azure—
somehow the names of the peoples
where I live are illegible
But we don't like to say *expunge*.
We don't like to say *obliterate*.
We don't like to say of ourselves, *settler*.

Thwarted water fights constraint
but river has been forced to become a lake.

II.
Once, the Siouxan language
mantled the land
from deep inside Canada
to Mississippi to this river basin.
Velvet mantle of Siouxan words
northern plains to delta south
to Atlantic woodlands.

My shape passes through this water
shedding its glove over and over again,
discards collapsing behind me.

a velvet mantle of things known and said

Say expunge
Say obliterate
Say settler.
Say, A settler, I walk my Jewish
white woman's body into the water

skin cell by skin cell
I enter the water.
my body taken in by water fallen from the sky
drop by drop, accumulated.

Inside the water I hear
and know I do not know
can never know enough.

Dam the rivers

I.
Eno, Haw
Reconnaissance
platter of the river basins

place
        placed
                placing
                        the heart beats
                                against the violence

a long time ago
                the heart

platter of river basins
replete with footprints   heartbeats
                        breath

a place

II.
contact
[not] examined

the settler reads land:
prehistoric   in other words *before him*

the settler picks and chooses history

what you can do to a place:
intrude
reconnoiter
monetize
settle   make to lie down

III.
to build a lake
graph paper

how

surface control
friction drag
catchlight
wake up
catch light

[not] examined

IV.
valleys
obliterated

bones dissolved into clay
breath and heartbeat
rise into clouds
above catchment of
earth movers

platter of river basins
replete with footprints and heartbeats

V.
hoarded in a laboratory
Sherds
assemblages
ceramic

the writers of white *history*
thwart the Eno and the Haw

VI.
today no print
in bones melted into silt

swimming water
remembers but cannot say
blood and spit and eye liquid

rise into the clouds

from clouds
replenish
the bowl
the basin
the bone colored platter

platter of the river basins
replete with footprints and heartbeats
defies reconfiguration

Found Poem

I wrote a poem in which
a Black minister walks with his ancestors.
It wasn't bad, my poem,
but the words were cherry picked from that Black minister
as if at the disposal of my purposes.
My poem was righteous, pleased with itself
        and it fit into my manuscript,
but the words were his, not mine

Snake Like a Wreath

Swimming, I look sideways and see a yellow and black snake, curled like a little wreath on the surface of the water. It uncoils and swims off, swift and brilliant. I'm nervous about swimming snakes, but seeing one makes the idea less frightening. I look up poisonous swimming snakes, but this little black and yellow beauty does not fit any of the pictures and descriptions, or so I think.

Hurricane Season, 2017

I.
pink stone
in my palm
heart beating
lake's pulse

banked clouds
foretell storms

water shivering crepe
sky blue sky gray sky white
mirrored in brown surface
russet weave

her depths shiver

tall man in blue cap swimming
angled arms
same man last year
same man   swimmer's stoop
without my glasses,
I know his shape
slap of arms
entering water
mark him

II.
thunder stone
shape of my thumb
bronze marled

paisley grainy
sonogram churns
voracious rotation over San Juan

minute bronze fastener
forestalls   thunderstone
unborn has made his choice

I walk in chest-deep
rufous   water
I run
hammer toes
flex and bear my weight
silt records no trace of me
in tree tops, the crows' hilarity
I lie down into the breast stroke
no gravity   none whatsoever
my body eases
through tea brown water

A solitary six or seven year old
dives and swims. Next to me, he is
talking through his goggles.
He doesn't like the waves.
I say the wind and the boats
have caused the chop.
Maybe the hurricane.
He says, *The boats can't help it,*
but the wind can.

He says his last name is wind
He says it is Dutch and I say my
father's family emigrated from Holland.
I ask the boy, Did he come with family.
He says, *Yes*, and gestures toward the beach.
He is here with his *oma* and his *opa*,
That's Dutch for grandma and grandpa, he says.

III.
creaking gate
      sound of children on swings
creaking gate
      air borne heron's call, neck crooked, feet dangling

rasping call
      earthly
      rude

wings open a rumor
wings brush aside the sky and open a portal

Autumn coming:
my childhood friend's dire disease;
an eight year old nearly lynched on a picnic bench
his abraded child's brown neck—
the chlorine saturated indoor pool in town

IV.
edges smartly fractured
leuco gneiss
bands this
river basin
nodes of red
mica glisten
magnetite black as
dried blood
resists
has held fast
has weathered rifts
out lasted failed rifts

river's rocks will be here
I will have
a new grandchild
and my daughter will
have returned from the dead

Schooled

I asked the lake what I should do

> prostrate yourself and feel the earth below your ear
> prostrate yourself and feel our loss
> prostrate yourself and receive
>
> feel from the earth's wet smell
> the lake will never cease to exist
> feel and you, too, will live forever

Winter

I miss the sky
I miss the water
enveloping me

I miss the paired sworn egrets
Disney spiral
glyph white glide
one about the other

I miss the teenage girls
trash talking
in water to their
not-woman shoulders

I miss carnitas grilling under the trees
scenting the egret air

I miss my body
under the sky
in the water

unbound

Faith S. Holsaert is a writer, activist, and teacher who lives with her partner Vicki Smith in Durham, North Carolina. Since 1979, her writing has appeared in *Redbook, Calyx, Prime Number Magazine*, and many others.

She has been nominated for a Pushcart Prize, and has been awarded the 2018 North Carolina Literary Review Albright Prize in nonfiction and the 2012 Press 53 Prize in the novella. She has written fiction since childhood, receiving an MFA in Fiction from the Warren Wilson Program for Writers.

Holsaert has been active since her teens, working as field staff with the Student Nonviolent Coordinating Committee (SNCC) and later in the coalfields of West Virginia where she raised her children.

In 2010, University of Illinois Press released *Hands on the Freedom Plow, Personal Accounts by Women in SNCC*, which Holsaert co-edited with five other women.

After working in fiction and occasional nonfiction all her life, Holsaert began to write poetry in workshops taught by Alexis Pauline Gumbs.

www.ingramcontent.com/pod-product-compliance
Lightning Source LLC
LaVergne TN
LVHW041600070426
835507LV00011B/1220